HOW TO
DEAL EFFECTIVELY WITH INAPPROPRIATE TALKING AND NOISEMAKING

Lee Kern
Gabriell Sacks

HOW TO IMPROVE CLASSROOM BEHAVIOR SERIES

SERIES EDITORS

Saul Axelrod
Steven C. Mathews

pro·ed
An International Publisher

8700 Shoal Creek Boulevard
Austin, Texas 78757-6897
800/897-3202   Fax 800/397-7633
www.proedinc.com

© 2003 by PRO-ED, Inc.
8700 Shoal Creek Boulevard
Austin, Texas 78757-6897
800/897-3202 Fax 800/397-7633
www.proedinc.com

Library of Congress Cataloging-in-Publication Data

Kern, Lee.
    How to deal effectively with inappropriate talking and noisemaking / Lee Kern and
Gabriell Sacks.
        p. cm.
    ISBN 0-89079-970-9
    1. Classroom management. 2. School children—Discipline.   3. Behavior modification.
4. Verbal behavior. I. Sacks, Gabriell. II. Title.

LB3013.K448 2004
371.102'4—dc21

                                                                          2003046778

This book is designed in Minion and Gill Sans.

Printed in the United States of America

1 2 3 4 5 6 7 8 9 10   07 06 05 04 03

CONTENTS

FOREWORD

Having spent several years as a classroom teacher, as a principal of both regular and special education students, and as an educational researcher, it has long been apparent to me that there is a need for materials that provide quick solutions to specific classroom problems. The *How To Improve Classroom Behavior Series,* edited by Saul Axelrod and Steven C. Mathews, fills that need. Although there have been a number of excellent research studies and texts that present effective classroom management techniques, the beauty of this series is that the authors have used their own experiences and surveyed the literature to present effective procedures that efficiently guide teachers toward solutions of common classroom management problems.

The value of such a series should be apparent. Teachers faced with particular problems, such as students who are disruptive or who bully or tease, can consult the series for solutions. Ideally these books will be found on a bookshelf in the teachers' lounge. Without having to search through professional journals or cumbersome texts, teachers will easily be able to focus on the particular behavior that is a topic of concern. Principals, school psychologists, counselors, and other professionals to whom teachers sometimes refer students with problem behaviors will also find these texts useful in providing solutions for teachers. It also should prove extremely helpful, especially to beginning teachers, when a principal or psychologist can provide a simple, uncluttered text that tells the teacher exactly what to do in certain problem situations.

The booklets in the series are presented in such a way that they help the user to clearly define the behavior of concern and then to implement step-by-step programs that deal effectively with that behavior. Because the booklets are written in straightforward, nontechnical language, teachers will not become bogged down in trying to understand psychological jargon or complex procedures.

Saul Axelrod is a respected researcher and author. He has published more than 60 research articles and book chapters on behavior and eight books that deal with classroom problems. An excellent writer, he has served on the editorial boards of 10 prominent psychological and educational journals. As a licensed psychologist and professor of special education, he has wide experience in instructing teachers in the use of classroom management techniques. Due to his extensive experience and many professional contacts, he and his coeditor were able to select authors well qualified to write each booklet in the series.

Steven C. Mathews is an educator who has spent more than 30 years in educational publishing, including stints as managing editor of education for the College Division of Allyn & Bacon and as editor in chief of PRO-ED. He served two terms as president of the Austin, Texas, Chapter of the Council for Exceptional Children and has served on advisory committees for the American Speech-Language-Hearing Association, Council for Learning Disabilities, and Texas Council for Exceptional Children. His publications include tests and therapy materials.

It has been my privilege to work closely with both Saul and Steve. I participated with Saul in several of his first research publications and coauthored with him my most recent publication. I know firsthand that he is an excellent researcher, teacher, and author. I know of no one better qualified to produce this series. I have also worked closely with Steve, who served as managing editor for a number of my publications, including my own *How To Manage Behavior Series*. His skill in guiding the selection of topics and in shaping and polishing manuscripts is unparalleled in my experience. Their cooperative efforts make this series a valuable contribution to the field of teacher education.

R. Vance Hall
Professor Emeritus
University of Kansas

PREFACE TO SERIES

The idea for the *How To Improve Classroom Behavior Series* grew from our conversations with R. Vance Hall. His popular series of booklets called *How To Manage Behavior* presents, in a step-by-step manner, behavioral procedures and techniques. Although they are practical and quick to read, the booklets in his series do not easily show a teacher who may be unfamiliar with behavioral techniques which ones would be best to use in specific situations. We agreed that a new series was needed—a series that would present behavioral techniques in booklets that each address a specific problem behavior that teachers encounter in their classrooms.

Development of the Series

We first wanted to determine what common behavior problems occur in the classroom. In reviewing the literature (Bender, 1987; Bibou-Nakou, Kiosseoglou, & Stogiannidou, 2000; Bickerstaff, Leon, & Hudson, 1997; Elam, 1987, 1989; Elam, Rose, & Gallup, 1994; Fagen, 1986; Gibbons & Jones, 1994; Greenlee & Ogletree, 1993; Jones, Quah, & Charlton, 1996; Malone, Bonitz, & Rickett, 1998; Mastrilli & Brown, 1999; Ordover, 1997), we found that common classroom behavior problems were consistently reported regardless of the age of the student, the type of classroom, the special needs of the student, the experience of the teacher, the passage of time, or the part of the world. This review produced a preliminary list of possible topics for the series.

The preliminary list was then compared to topics presented in textbooks used in courses on behavior management and classroom discipline (e.g., Charles, 1999; Kaplan, 1995, 2000; Sloane, 1988; Walker & Walker, 1991; Workman & Katz, 1995). The list was also evaluated by educators and psychologists from university and other school settings. Their input helped us create a revised list of topics.

The final list of topics, reflected in the titles of the *How To Improve Classroom Behavior Series,* was created by combining topics that had common themes and eliminating topics that did not lend themselves to the format of the series. After the final list was completed, we contacted potential authors for each booklet. Each author selected has a background related to the topic, knowledge of current behavioral principles, and experience working directly with teachers and students.

Format of the Series

All the booklets in the series were written in the same format. Each booklet includes the following:

- Practical and nontechnical information
- All the information a teacher needs to implement a strategy
- Step-by-step strategy presentation
- Numerous strategy suggestions from which the reader can choose
- Numerous examples of various levels of problem severity, ages of students, and instructional settings
- Interactive learning procedures with space and prompts for the reader to make oral or written responses
- References and suggestions for further readings

Uses of the Series

Each of the booklets in the series may be used independently or in conjunction with the other booklets. Each can be read and the information used by regular classroom teachers, special education teachers, teachers in collaborative classrooms, school psychologists, and anyone else who has students who exhibit the behavior that is the topic of the booklet.

The design of the booklets allows them to be used without additional information. However, they also lend themselves to workshop, in-service, or consultation situations. They are ideal for a special education teacher, school psychologist, or other consultant to share with a teacher who requests information or who reports a problem in her or his classroom.

Acknowledgments

We would first like to thank our friend R. Vance Hall for his advice, counsel, and patience, and for writing the foreword to the series. The series would not exist without Vance's contributions.

We would also like to thank the contributors to the series. They all have prepared manuscripts following a prescribed format in a very short period of time. The many people at PRO-ED who have contributed to the series from its inception through its publication also have earned our thanks and respect.

Saul Axelrod and
Steven C. Mathews
Series Editors

Series References

Bender, W. N. (1987). Correlates of classroom behavior problems among learning disabled and nondisabled children in mainstream classes. *Learning Disabilities Quarterly, 10,* 317–324.

Bibou-Nakou, I., Kiosseoglou, G., & Stogiannidou, A. (2000). Elementary teacher's perceptions regarding school behavior problems: Implications for school psychological services. *Psychology in the Schools, 37,* 123–134.

Bickerstaff, S., Leon, S. H., & Hudson, J. G. (1997). Preserving the opportunity for education: Texas' alternative education programs for disruptive youth. *Journal of Law and Education, 26,* 1–39.

Charles, C. M. (1999). *Building classroom discipline* (6th ed.). New York: Longman.

Elam, S. M. (1987). Differences between educators and the public on questions of education policy. *Phi Delta Kappan, 69,* 294–296.

Elam, S. M. (1989). The second Gallup/Phi Delta Kappa poll of teachers' attitudes toward the public schools. *Phi Delta Kappan, 70,* 785–798.

Elam, S. M., Rose, L. C., & Gallup, A. M. (1994). The 26th annual Phi Delta Kappa/Gallup poll of the public's attitude toward the public schools. *Phi Delta Kappan, 76,* 41–56.

Fagen, S. A. (1986). Least intensive interventions for classroom behavior problems. *Pointer, 31,* 21–28.

Gibbons, L., & Jones, L. (1994). *Novice teachers' reflectivity upon their classroom management.* (ERIC Documentation Reproduction Service No. ED386446)

Greenlee, A. R., & Ogletree, E. J. (1993). *Teachers' attitude toward student discipline problems and classroom management strategies.* (ERIC Documentation Reproduction Service No. ED364330)

Jones, K., Quah, M. L., & Charlton, T. (1996). Behaviour which primary and special school teachers in Singapore find most troublesome. *Research in Education, 55,* 62–73.

Kaplan, J. S. (1995). *Beyond behavior modification: A cognitive–behavioral approach to behavior management in the school* (3rd ed.). Austin, TX: PRO-ED.

Kaplan, J. S. (2000). *Beyond functional assessment: A social–cognitive approach to the evaluation of behavior problems in children and youth.* Austin, TX: PRO-ED.

Malone, B. G., Bonitz, D. A., & Rickett, M. M. (1998). Teacher perceptions of disruptive behavior: Maintaining instructional focus. *Educational Horizons, 76,* 189–194.

Mastrilli, T. M., & Brown, D. S. (1999). Elementary student teachers' cases: An analysis of dilemmas and solutions. *Action in Teacher Education, 21,* 50–60.

Ordover, E. (1997). *Inclusion of students with disabilities who are labeled "disruptive": Issues papers for legal advocates and parents.* Boston: Center for Law and Education.

Sloane, H. N. (1988). *The good kid book: How to solve the 16 most common behavior problems.* Champaign, IL: Research Press.

Walker, H. M., & Walker, J. E. (1991). *Coping with noncompliance in the classroom: A positive approach for teachers.* Austin, TX: PRO-ED.

Workman, E. A., & Katz, A. M. (1995). *Teaching behavioral self-control to students* (2nd ed.). Austin, TX: PRO-ED.

How To Improve Classroom Behavior Series

How To Deal Effectively with Inappropriate Talking and Noisemaking

How To Deal Effectively with Lying, Stealing, and Cheating

How To Deal Effectively with Whining and Tantrum Behaviors

How To Deal with Students Who Challenge and Defy Authority

How To Help Students Complete Classwork and Homework Assignments

How To Help Students Follow Directions, Pay Attention, and Stay on Task

How To Help Students Play and Work Together

How To Help Students Remain Seated

How To Prevent and Safely Manage Physical Aggression and Property Destruction

Introduction

Few things are more frustrating for a classroom teacher than to be standing in front of her or his class trying to give directions or teach a lesson while students are talking or calling out. Imagine Ms. Lopez, a new sixth-grade science teacher at Hawthorne Elementary School who is eager to begin a new unit with her class about vertebrates. In the summer she had gone to a workshop about how to make science lessons more interactive and exciting, and she is looking forward to starting the new unit. She walks to the front of the class, expects that students will quiet down, and commences to explain the introductory activity. Although some students have stopped talking and looked up at the teacher, several students in the back have continued conversations about weekend plans with their friends. Ms. Lopez is becoming frustrated because it appears that no one is listening. The quiet students are becoming impatient because they can't hear the teacher. The noisy students, unaware that their attention is needed, are oblivious that they are missing important instructions. What did Ms. Lopez do wrong? How could she have gotten all her students' attention, quieted the talking, and begun her lesson without feeling frustrated?

When students disrupt a class by making distracting noises, talking at inappropriate times, or blurting out answers, teachers cannot teach effectively, and students miss important information. Teaching students when and how to refrain from talking, making noises, or calling out is an important instructional component that is often overlooked. The necessary skills to quiet a class should be in every teacher's repertoire. This booklet is designed to help teachers manage students' talking and maintain acceptable noise levels in their classrooms, and to implement effective rules for talking in other areas of the school.

Part I of this booklet describes when talking is acceptable and when quiet is necessary. Suggestions are given for teaching students how to ask permission to talk and how to use appropriate voice levels. Part II discusses how to establish and teach rules for talking or noise-making in settings other than the classroom. For example, the type of talking allowed in the hallways between classes is different from the type of talking allowed in the cafeteria during lunch or in the auditorium during an assembly. Part III describes classwide interventions to reduce disruptive talking or noisemaking in the classroom. These are simple techniques teachers can use to maintain acceptable noise levels in the classroom and curtail inappropriate talking. Finally, Part IV discusses individual interventions that can be used to discourage disruptive talking or noisemaking with students who may not respond to more general interventions.

PART I:
Establishing General
Guidelines for Talking

When Talking Is Acceptable
and When Quiet Is Necessary

Humans are social creatures. It is no surprise, then, that students are eager to socialize and talk during school. The key, however, is to teach students about when talking is acceptable and what volume level is appropriate. In Mr. Frank's 10th-grade social studies class, students know that when they are working in small groups they are expected to talk in working voices. Indoor voices are acceptable for students giving presentations. Silence is expected when Mr. Frank speaks to the class or independent seatwork is required.

At the beginning of the year, Mr. Frank taught his students that "working voices" means talking in a whisper so that only the person next to you can hear. "Indoor voices" are a little louder so that a larger group can hear. "Silence" means absolutely no talking or noisemaking. Mr. Frank also has a large poster of a traffic signal in his classroom that serves as a visual reminder to the students to be aware of the volume of their voices. Each light color signifies the voice level that is appropriate for the activity: A red signal means "silence," yellow means "working voices," and green means "indoor voices." At the beginning of an activity, Mr. Frank flicks the overhead lights in the classroom as a signal for students to look at the poster. He then walks over to the poster, chooses the appropriate signal color for the activity, and places the colored circle on the traffic signal. He gives a verbal reminder such as, "This small-group activity is a yellow signal, so please use working voices."

There are many situations in the classroom or school when it is necessary for students to be silent. For example, Mr. Frank expects students to be silent when he is giving instructions or teaching a lesson or when a student is doing a presentation. When the traffic light signal is red, his students know this means "silence." At the beginning of the year, Mr. Frank practiced silence with his students and discussed what silence meant. He started with a brainstorming activity by asking his students to list all the words or activities they associated with silence. The students came up with words such as *quiet, restful, meditation, attentive, boring, peaceful,* and *uncomfortable.* They gave examples of when and why silence would be necessary, such as, "When the teacher is giving directions," "During an assembly," and "When a classmate is giving a presentation." The class role-played various scenarios and discussed the consequences of talking when silence was demanded. For example, Mr. Frank gave a group of four students a card that said, "The teacher is giving directions." One student in the group played the teacher while two others talked to each other and the third listened quietly. The whole class then discussed what happened. How did the teacher feel? What did the quiet student learn? What did the two talking students miss? Mr. Frank followed a similar procedure for the yellow (working voices) and green (indoor voices) signals.

Ms. Yoo teaches a kindergarten class of 21 students that includes two special education students with Down syndrome. She had to devise a method for signaling students about their talking that was simple and easy to follow. She decided to use a bell. One chime meant "silence—no talking—wait for teacher instruction." Two chimes meant "quiet talking—free play or group work." Ms. Yoo gave many examples and nonexamples of each condition and had her students role-play different scenarios. She also gave her class ample opportunities throughout the school day to respond to the bell signals, especially at the beginning of the year or following holidays. As a visual reminder, Ms. Yoo made a poster depicting the bell and what one or two chimes meant, and she often gave a verbal reminder after ringing the bell.

Question 1

> How do students know what type of talking is acceptable in your classroom?

_____

_____

_____

_____

_____

_____

_____

_____

How To Get Permission To Talk

It is useful to have a classroom procedure for students to get permission to talk. In a large class, a student raising his or her hand is usually a signal to the teacher that the student has something to say. But students must learn to wait to be called on. Simply raising their hand and then proceeding to talk is not acceptable. Students often need to practice these routines at the beginning of the year until they are familiar with them. Reminders throughout the year can ensure that all students adhere to the routines. In smaller classrooms, students can be taught to wait for a pause in the conversation before they begin to talk. This important social skill teaches students to not interrupt conversations. However, this skill needs to be practiced in order for students to become aware of the flow of conversations and the appropriate times to join in. At the beginning of the school year, students will often need to rehearse these procedures. This can be done through role plays and practice sessions or during the course of daily activities. It is also important for the teacher to provide consequences in the form of praise or some other type of reward for following the procedures. For example, Ms. West allows her junior high school students 5 minutes of free time at the end of physics class if they refrain from talking out throughout the period. Providing a rewarding consequence increases the likelihood that students will continue to follow the rules. Reminding students about the rule may be necessary too, especially at the beginning of the year and after holidays. As the school year progresses, most students should follow the procedures consistently.

There are times when practice, reminders, and rewarding consequences do not result in students routinely following the rules. When this happens, it is necessary to add some sort of consequence for failing to follow the rules. If many students are having difficulty following the procedures, it is beneficial to have a class discussion about the problem. If only one student or a few students cannot follow the procedures, consequences can be applied individually. Consequences might include reminding the student the first time the rule is broken, having the student write out the rule and put it on her or his desk the second time the rule is broken, and having the student miss 5 minutes of recess for the third transgression. It is important to apply consequences consistently. This means that the consequence should be predictable to students and should be applied for *every* transgression. One of the biggest mistakes a teacher can make is to ignore or excuse less serious transgressions. This will only lead to behavior escalations, and soon the classroom will be out of control.

It should be noted that a student sometimes fails to adhere to rules in spite of ample teaching and consistent consequences. This suggests that the student may be lacking skills or self-control. In this case, it is important to develop a more intensive individualized intervention, as described in Part IV, Individual Interventions.

Question 2

> How do students in your classroom get permission to talk? What
> happens when they do not follow the rules?

_____

_____

_____

_____

Appropriate Talking for the Setting

Within the school, different settings place varying demands on students. It is important for students to know exactly what is expected of
them in each setting. Not all types of talking are appropriate in every
setting within a school. For example, the students at West Middle
School know that during recess it is appropriate for them to socialize
and talk to their friends about plans for the weekend. They also know
that "outdoor voices," including yelling, are acceptable on the playground. Likewise, the students know that during a class activity in language arts, the only talking that is acceptable is discussion about the
activity in "whisper voices."

It is important for students to practice different types and levels
of talking in each different setting. Students should be given examples
and nonexamples of the types of talking that are allowed in various
settings. Teachers should point out to students when they are talking
appropriately and when they are too loud or off task. At the beginning
of the year, Ms. Carter took her fifth graders on a tour of the school. She
stopped at various places around the school and discussed with her
class the appropriate type of talking for the area. In the auditorium,
Ms. Carter had her fifth graders practice being silent and attentive. They
discussed why silence and attentiveness were appropriate in the auditorium. Likewise, she stopped in the hallway, in the cafeteria, in the li-

brary, and on the playground, demonstrating the appropriate type of talking at each stop. Back in her classroom, Ms. Carter discussed the different types of activities the class would be doing throughout the year. She had her students define the appropriate type of talking for each type of activity. She also had her students come up with a good consequence for students who consistently follow the rules and a different consequence for those who do not follow the rules. Her students decided that lunch with the teacher on a monthly basis would be a special treat for those who followed the rules. They also decided that for students who did not follow the rules, the following consequences were appropriate: a reminder for the first transgression, losing 5 minutes of recess to discuss the problem with Ms. Carter for the second transgression, and a note home for the third transgression. If these general procedures are not adequate, a setting intervention can be developed, as described in Part II, Specific Setting Interventions.

Question 3

Name three settings in your school and describe what type of talking is appropriate in each.

a. _____

b. _____

c. _____

Conclusion

Most students love to talk, and schools provide ample opportunities for students to socialize throughout the day. However, it is important that students know when talking is acceptable and when it is not. Certain types of talking can enhance students' learning, such as small-group discussions focused on a specific project. However, other types of talking can be an impediment to students' success, such as when students talk or call out during a lesson. Methods for teaching students appropriate talking and for obtaining quiet in the classroom should be in every teacher's repertoire.

PART II:
Specific Setting Interventions

Matching Intervention to the Setting

Schools are composed of a number of specific settings outside the classroom where students congregate for various activities. Some of these specific settings are characterized by structured activities or routines; others are unstructured and consist of student-selected or student-generated activities. For example, the cafeteria at lunchtime is a structured setting in which the routine includes students entering in an orderly fashion, obtaining and consuming lunch, disposing of materials and trash, and exiting at the proper time. In contrast, the gym, as a designated location where students can spend their free time after lunch, may represent an unstructured setting in which students have the option of socializing, being alone, or engaging in a number of available activities. These types of settings require a continuum of student independence and self-control that usually exceeds the classroom setting. Thus, it is critical that students learn the expectations and skills necessary to function effectively in various school settings.

There are several settings within schools in which staff commonly report having problems with noise or inappropriate talking. For example, the cafeteria, hallway, and student locker area are usually described as problematic settings in schools. Therefore, the first step for intervention development is for staff to identify settings where unacceptable levels of problems occur. These can be identified by reports from volunteers regularly assigned to a specific setting, high rates of disciplinary actions associated with a particular setting, or student complaints of inappropriate comments or behavior by fellow students.

Question 4

> Describe the specific settings in your school where excessive or inappropriate talking and noisemaking occur.

a. _____

_____

What information helped you identify these settings?

b. _____

_____

When designing interventions for specific settings, it is important to keep in mind that each setting within a school is unique. Therefore, each setting requires a corresponding intervention that is matched to the expectations within that setting. This does not mean that an entirely distinctive intervention needs to be developed for each different setting within a school. Rather, universal rules should be developed that can be applied in slightly different ways to address the needs of each setting. For example, students may be taught to use appropriate voice levels. Rules can then be added if the universal rules are not adequate.

Question 5

> What is a universal rule that is appropriate for your school?

a. _____

How should this rule be applied to one of the specific settings that you identified as problematic in Question 4?

b. _____

_____

Teaching the Setting Expectations

Ensuring that students behave in a manner appropriate in all school settings is more complex than it initially appears. Three important issues need to be considered when teaching specific setting expectations. First, because students adhere to the rules in one setting (e.g., the classroom) does not mean they will automatically adhere to the rules in a different setting (e.g., the cafeteria). Settings differ in ways that challenge the most skilled teacher. For example, unlike the classroom that is teacher directed and controlled, less structured settings are often dominated by peer feedback and expectations. The influence of peers often has a considerable impact on the way students behave, particularly as they grow into adolescents. Second, when left on their own, many students (particularly younger ones) are unable to structure their time, even if they are able to conform to a classroom structure developed by their teacher. Third, students sometimes cannot transfer or apply rules that they learn in one setting to other settings. What follows are procedures that will increase the likelihood of desired behavior across school settings.

It is helpful if schoolwide rules are already established. Schoolwide rules are generally written broadly to reflect behavioral expectations across settings. For example, typical schoolwide rules may include "Be Respectful," "Keep Your Hands and Feet to Yourself," "Be Ready," "Be Responsible," and "Follow Directions." These broad rules can accommodate expectations that are idiosyncratic to each specific setting. If schoolwide rules are not in place, the teacher can develop broad rules for the students in his or her classroom. Additional rules to address problems in specific settings can supplement broad rules. For example, although schoolwide rules were in place at Sherman High School, the cafeteria workers were concerned about the length of time it took to serve lunch to the students. Students were socializing in line, which caused an inefficient procession through the line, and cafeteria workers were often unable to hear food orders because of the noise level. Numerous attempts by cafeteria workers and monitors to quiet the students were unsuccessful. Thus, an additional rule was established for the cafeteria that stated, "Be Silent Until You Exit the Food Line." After the rule was implemented, a volunteer was assigned to monitor the line for 2 weeks. Students who talked in line were asked to go to the end of the line. Because this consequence delayed their free time following lunch, students quickly learned to remain quiet.

After rules for specific settings have been established, they must be taught to students. Rule teaching requires not only describing the rules but also providing instruction in how the rules should be applied in each setting. To help students fully understand the setting expectations, a number of approaches, such as didactic instruction, modeling, role playing, and completing rule-related activities, can be used. For example, because the students in Ms. Xin's kindergarten class had not previously experienced any particular school setting, she created several activities to help her students learn the rule "Walk Quietly in the Halls During Class Time." First, she described the rule to the students and posted it in the classroom. She then modeled walking quietly through the halls. After modeling quiet walking, she selected dyads of students to do role plays. Some dyads were instructed to role-play quiet walking, while other dyads were instructed to whisper, whistle, hum, or make stomping noises with their feet. After each dyad's role play, the rest of the class voted whether the dyad followed or did not follow the rule. Finally, Ms. Xin had each kindergartner draw a picture showing himself or herself following the rule.

Teachers often end rule instruction at this point. However, practicing the expected behavior in context with reminders and feedback has been shown to make a dramatic difference in how well students adhere to rules. Students often are able to describe and model behavior consistent with a specific rule, yet they fail to follow the rule in the setting in which it is expected. This may happen because the role play did not specifically capture situations that occur in a certain setting. For example, Ms. Xin's class may walk quietly in the hallways when they are alone during practice time, but when they pass Mr. Winter's unruly fifth-grade class goofing off, they want to join in the game playing. Or students may be distracted in busy environments and forget about a rule. Regardless of the reasons, good behavior should be practiced in context, and reminders and feedback should be provided. For example, numerous teachers at Lakeside Middle School reported overhearing inappropriate language while students waited outside for the afternoon bus to arrive. Although the students received instruction and practice in the rule "Be Respectful," the inappropriate language continued. A school volunteer charged with monitoring adherence to the rule at the bus stop reminded the students of the rule as soon as students arrived, stating that it included use of only appropriate language. After every 1 minute or 2 minutes in which all language was appropriate, she praised the students on their appropriate language. In addition, she distributed tokens for weekly school drawings (described later) to students who were observed to be particularly respectful. Whenever she heard language that was not appropriate, she provided feedback by telling the student that the language he or she had just used was not appropriate.

Question 6

What are the three steps for teaching expectations for specific settings?

a. _____

_____

b. _____

_____

c. _____

_____

Rewarding Appropriate Behavior

Unlike the classroom, specific settings in the school tend to be subject to less supervision. As a result, students receive fewer rewards for appropriate behavior than they would in the classroom of a positive and encouraging teacher. This is unfortunate because behavior that is rewarded will continue to occur or increase in frequency. This factor alone may account for the disproportionate number of problems that occur in specific settings outside the classroom. Designing a simple reward system can correct this predicament.

Because it is virtually impossible to monitor the behavior of *all* students in a specific setting, it is most efficient to set up a system to randomly reward acts of good behavior. For example, the recess monitors at Hillcrest Elementary School dispense up to 25 "Caught You" cards daily to students they catch behaving appropriately. When a student earns 5 Caught You cards, he or she may visit the office to select a reward from the treasure chest. The students at Guadalupe Elementary School earn happy-face stickers for appropriate behavior throughout the school. The student with the most happy-face stickers at the end of the week is taken out to lunch by the principal. At Sentinal Middle School, staff members administer "Good Sense" cards in the hallways, cafeteria, locker area, and quad. The Good Sense cards are deposited in a bin for a weekly drawing, and the student whose name is drawn may select from a number of items donated by the surrounding community, such as movie passes, pizza coupons, and gift certificates. Each month, staff members at Walden High School select two students who exhibit excellent behavior throughout school settings for model citizenship awards. A monthly award ceremony is held, and parents are notified of the award and invited to the ceremony.

A few important points should be kept in mind when developing reward systems. First, rewards must be preferred and powerful enough that students want to earn them. For example, school supplies may not be a good reward for students who do not like school. This issue can usually be addressed by offering an array of rewards so that students have options and can select something they want. Second, students often tire of specific rewards. Their interest can be enhanced by periodically introducing novel rewards. Finally, rewards must be age appropriate. Although elementary-age students may enjoy lunch with the principal, high school students generally prefer to be with their peers. Likewise, extended lunchtime may be a powerful reward for a high school student in an open campus situation, but it is not appropriate for elementary-age students who need supervision or who cannot afford to miss instruction.

Question 7

Describe three factors that can influence the success of a reward system.

a. _____

b. _____

c. _____

Responding to Inappropriate Behavior

Consequences for responding to problem behavior come in a variety of forms. In general, it is best to select consequences that are logically related to the infraction or that are instructive. For example, a related consequence for a student who uses inappropriate language at recess is to have the student write a letter of apology to peers. An instructive consequence is to have the student generate several appropriate statements expressing the same content expressed in the statement containing inappropriate language (e.g., You're not following the rules, so I don't want to play with you). Likewise, if a student is unable to keep his or her voice volume at a low level in the cafeteria, a related consequence would be to have the student eat silently the following day. An instructive consequence would be to have the student write five ways he or she could remember to keep noise at a low level. Consequences that are logically related to the infraction or are instructive to the student are more likely to be acceptable because they make sense to students, and they teach students alternative, appropriate ways to respond in similar situations.

It is important to predetermine the consequence for specific rule infractions for two reasons. First, because multiple individuals are often responsible for monitoring a specific setting (e.g., teachers rotate recess or lunchroom duty so they have the responsibility only once a week), consequences for rule infractions should be preestablished and be applied consistently to students by all staff members. In addition, predetermined consequences can be clearly described to students. When the consequence is known, it sometimes acts as a deterrent for students.

They are less likely to rebel if they are already informed as to what will happen.

Question 8

> What are the advantages of consequences that are logically related to the infraction or are instructive to the student?

_____

_____

_____

The Importance of Surveillance

Student misbehavior occurs more frequently in areas without surveillance because of the absence of rewards and consequences. Thus, blueprints for school surveillance must be established across school settings. Surveillance is necessary not only for preventing problems but also for providing prompts and consequences for rules within specific school settings. The easiest approach to ensure surveillance is to assign a specific staff member or volunteer to monitor a specific setting. It is important that the individual fully understands the expectations and consequences and that reminders are provided to the students. Some schools use responsible students, such as hall monitors, to perform this duty. They must understand the expectations and prompt good behavior, and a procedure must be in place for providing consequences that includes backup and follow-through from staff members. If staff availability prohibits regular assignment of monitors or the school lacks the organization and structure to establish a process, teachers can provide impromptu surveillance. For example, Ms. Rockwell works in a high school with a very inexperienced principal. The principal has not established schoolwide rules, and Ms. Rockwell has noticed increasing problems in the hallways between classes. Thus, she convened a group of teachers to help solve the problem. The group of teachers decided they would adjust their routines slightly so they could provide additional surveillance between class times. Typically, they waited until class began and the halls quieted to travel to the teacher lounge or copy room. Instead, they decided they would surveil during the break between classes, watching for good behavior as well as infractions. Each day the teachers took a different route to ensure that all areas of the building were monitored.

Question 9

How can good surveillance in specific school settings reduce problems?

Conclusion

Problems within a school, including inappropriate talking and noise-making, can often be traced to specific school settings. It is important to identify problematic settings and to intervene in those settings. Effective intervention, if properly implemented, can make school a safe and positive environment for students and staff members.

PART III:
Classwide Interventions

Establishing Classroom Expectations

A noisy classroom is extremely frustrating to a teacher. Noisy classrooms interfere with learning and instruction. However, students usually are not noisy at the beginning of a school year. The noise level in a classroom tends to increase gradually over time when expectations are not made clear. Thus, it is best to establish expectations at the start of a school year and adhere to them throughout the term. However, it is not too late to make a change if noise level has become a problem during the school year.

In addition to interventions for specific settings, it is important to teach students classroom expectations. This includes identifying activities when talking is not permitted (e.g., independent seatwork, when another person is talking) and teaching an acceptable voice volume when talking is permitted.

In addition to teaching the acceptable level of noise, the content of appropriate talk needs to be specified. Classrooms should be constructive environments where students help and learn from one another. Students need to be taught how to make supportive and encouraging statements and how to provide constructive feedback. Specific instruction accompanied by modeling and role playing, as described in Part II, Specific Setting Interventions, can help students learn these skills.

Once expectations are established and taught, teachers must strictly adhere to the expectations. It is often tempting for teachers to begin a lesson when students are mostly quiet. This is not a good practice and will only lead to trouble (i.e., more talking). If the expectation is that students work quietly, instruction should not begin until *all* students are quiet. Students will learn quickly that the expectations will be enforced.

Physical Arrangement

The physical layout of a classroom can have a great influence on student behavior. There are three features of the classroom arrangement that will help to reduce talking and noise when a quiet classroom is needed. The first is student proximity. A seating arrangement where students are close to one another encourages interaction. Conversely, physical separation among students will decrease the classroom noise level. For example, individual desks allow for more student separation than tables. Likewise, when all desks face the front of the classroom, students are less likely to distract each other than when desks face one another. Most teachers have flexible desk arrangements that can be rearranged to suit each activity. Individual desks can be arranged together in clusters for group work and separated for quiet work.

The second classroom feature that influences student behavior is teacher observation and proximity. A teacher's desk in the far back corner of a classroom will not allow for ample surveillance. Classroom arrangements should always provide the opportunity for a teacher to observe *all* students in the classroom. Knowing the teacher may be watching will discourage students from inappropriate behavior. Also, close teacher proximity tends to reduce inappropriate student behavior. Teachers who remain at their desks are likely to have students who are talkative, off task, and disruptive. A teacher who periodically wanders around the classroom will encourage students to quietly engage in their work. In addition, walking around the classroom provides a teacher with the perfect opportunity to compliment students who are working quietly.

The third classroom feature that will help to maintain a quiet environment is the designation of a quiet area where a student who is easily distracted or highly disruptive can be sent. A study carrel is an ideal location for minimal distractions. If a carrel is not available, a corner of the classroom separated from other students will suffice. This area can be made available to students on request, because many students request a quiet area to help them stay on task and quietly complete their work.

Question 10

List three physical features of a classroom that will reduce unwanted noise.

a. _____

b. _____

c. _____

Preventive Measures

Although it is important to teach classroom expectations, it is equally important to remember that few problems happen in organized and structured classrooms where students are kept busy with interesting work. There are many classroom circumstances that increase the likelihood of problems, including a boring curriculum, unclear expectations, or too much down time. Under such conditions, students will busy themselves by chatting, socializing, or engaging in more serious infractions.

One strategy to prevent problems is to ensure that the curriculum is meaningful and challenging. For example, the following activities occurred daily during Ms. McCann's seventh-grade science class. Each class began with a teacher lecture, followed by students reading a chapter in their textbooks and then answering the end-of-chapter questions. At the end of each class, students exchanged papers and graded each other's questions. Ms. McCann noticed that she was having a difficult time keeping her students engaged and working quietly. She decided to try some curriculum changes. The students were about to begin a unit on recycling. Rather than her typical format of chapter reading and question answering, she developed an activity for each lesson. The first lesson focused on identifying items that could be recycled. Prior to the lesson, she asked her students to make a list of 10 items in their household that could be recycled. At the beginning of class, she had students form small groups to compare their lists and categorize them (e.g., paper goods, plastic items). The students were instructed to use their books as a resource to make sure that the items could be recycled and that each item fell into the appropriate category. After this small-group activity, the students convened as a class and compiled a master list of recyclable items. The students were then provided phone books to locate a recycling facility in their neighborhood. Their homework assignment was to contact the facility to obtain information about its recycling practices. Ms. McCann found that her students' engagement and interest in classwork greatly increased when they worked on activities that had personal meaning to them. At the same time, she was able to maintain the objectives developed for the seventh-grade science curriculum.

A second important preventive measure is to make sure that students fully understand classroom routines and lesson instructions. In Ms. Chew's reading class, she posted the daily schedule on the board. For example, on Monday students practiced their vocabulary words with partners during the first 5 minutes of class, then they convened in their reading groups for structured activities that were led by a designated student. This was followed by independent seatwork. When students were finished with their independent assignments, they engaged in silent leisure reading. At the beginning of class, the teacher reviewed the daily schedule and expectations for each activity. She also prepared students for a new independent activity by modeling the requirements and checking their accuracy on the first several problems. Posting the scheduled activities and checking to make sure students understood the instructions ensured that the class ran smoothly and without unwanted noise and disruption.

A final preventive approach is to make stimulating activities available to students when they have finished their assigned work. Talking and other disruptive behaviors often occur when students have completed their work and have nothing else to do. Making a variety of fun activities available to students after they have completed their work will encourage them to work diligently on assignments that may be less preferred and will keep them engaged after they have finished their assigned work.

Question 11

Describe three ways to prevent behavior problems in the classroom.

a. _____

b. _____

c. _____

Providing Simple Reminders

In spite of explicit and clear teaching of expectations and a good curriculum, it often takes time for students to learn classroom expectations. In addition, students sometimes become excited or concerned about an assignment or event in their personal lives and forget about classroom rules. It is wise, therefore, to develop a few simple reminders that will serve as universal messages for students. For example, a palm-out gesture can be used as a signal when a student or small group of students is getting too noisy. Teachers sometimes sound a bell or flash the classroom lights as a signal that the class has become too noisy. It is important for students to understand exactly what they should do when the signal is given.

Question 12

> What is a signal you could use in the classroom to remind students to be quiet?

Making Smooth Transitions

Transitions between activities or classes are often chaotic, filled with unacceptable noise and activity levels, and can be difficult for several reasons. Sometimes the expectations during or following a transition are unclear to students. Transitions also may be difficult because they require students to calm down after a period of social or physical activity. Finally, some students simply have difficulty with activity changes.

Teachers can make sure transitions are smooth by establishing a few routines and procedures. For example, at the end of a lesson, students should know where to deposit their assignments and how to prepare for the upcoming activity. Mr. Ray has his students place completed work in a basket, clear their desks, and wait quietly in their seats for the next lesson to begin. When it is time to transition to lunch in the cafeteria, Ms. White has her students clear their desks and sit quietly until she calls them, table by table, to line up quietly at the door. Mr. Bird's first-grade students have a difficult time transitioning from morning recess to reading time. Thus, after the bell rings, he plays calming music for 3 minutes, during which time his students can quietly get a drink at the fountain or rest their heads on their desks. As soon as the music stops, the students must gather their reading materials and silently transition to their reading groups.

It may be that routines and procedures are needed at the start of a new activity as well as during the transition. For example, Ms. Mendoza noticed that it took more than 5 minutes for her high school geometry students to get to class, quiet down, and have their materials ready so she could begin her lesson. Therefore, she instituted a new routine whereby students were given 10 review problems to complete during the first 5 minutes of class. The students were also given bonus points for completing the problems. Students began arriving to class on time and settling down to work so they could earn their bonus points. This routine set a work tone for the remainder of the class, provided useful review for the students, and avoided wasting valuable class time.

It is important that transition routines are practiced when they are first introduced. This will involve monitoring routines closely until all students adhere to them. Students should be lavishly praised for following a routine or making progress toward following a routine. It is also important to respond accordingly when students deviate from the routine. If only one or two students fail to follow the routine, it is most efficient to deal with them individually. Individual intervention procedures are described in Part IV, Individual Interventions. However, if several students in the class digress from the routine, it is best to implement an intervention with the entire class. Two effective procedures are known as *simple correction* and *positive practice overcorrection.* Simple correction requires the class to redo a transition that was not done appropriately. For example, Ms. White's class did not line up quietly at the door for lunch. She therefore required the students to take their seats and line up again. During positive practice overcorrection, students are required to practice the transition several times. Specifically, to implement a positive practice procedure, Ms. White might have her students practice quietly lining up for lunch five times rather than only once.

Timing is an important consideration when employing simple correction and positive practice overcorrection. These practice procedures are only effective if they are done during activities that students enjoy so that they are likely to learn and adhere to acceptable procedures rapidly. For example, Ms. White's students remained quiet through the transition practice because they were eager to get to the lunchroom. Had she implemented the practice procedures during math class, she most likely would not have witnessed such rapid results.

Question 13

> What is the difference between simple correction and positive practice overcorrection?

Increasing Active Engagement To Reduce Calling Out

Group activities in which students must wait to be called on present another occasion that can be associated with unwanted noise or calling out. Many students have not yet learned the self-control skills needed to wait until they are called on. It may also be the case that students are very eager to share their knowledge when asked a question. In addition, answering a question correctly is usually greeted with positive teacher and peer acknowledgment, making it a rewarding proposition. Finally, waiting in a group while students are called on individually is often very boring. All of these reasons may make students prone to call out.

One approach to avoid calling out is to make sure that students have the opportunity for active responding. This means that opportunities for *all* students to respond should be arranged as frequently as possible. Several different strategies allow for simultaneous responding by all students. Choral responding is one strategy in which students, as a group, orally respond to questions posed by the teacher. For example, Ms. Brown has her fourth graders recite multiplication tables in unison at the beginning of each math class.

Miniature chalkboards or dry-erase slates provide an opportunity for students to be actively engaged while simultaneously using a written format. Students can respond to complex math problems, spelling words, or science formulas this way. For example, Mr. Rice writes algebra problems on the board, and each student copies and answers the problem and then holds up his or her slate. Mr. Rice can then rapidly check for accurate responses. This activity keeps all students actively engaged, provides them with an optimal amount of practice, and provides them with immediate feedback on the accuracy of their answers.

Another approach is to provide each student with a set of cards with preprinted answers. For example, Ms. Key's American history students practice for their quizzes using preprinted *true* and *false* cards. She reads aloud a list of history facts, such as "World War I began in 1925," to which students respond by holding up either their true or false card. She then provides the correct response immediately for students to self-correct. Structuring opportunities for all students to actively respond not only reduces classroom problems by keeping students engaged but also improves academic performance by providing additional practice and review for all students.

Question 14

Describe a strategy to ensure that students are actively engaged.

Group Interventions

In spite of a teacher's best preventive efforts, it is sometimes necessary to introduce a behavior management strategy specifically designed to reduce excessive classroom noise and talking. It is best to begin with a reinforcement-based approach in which students are taught and then rewarded for good behavior. There are two ways that a system can be set up to address the behavior of the classroom as a whole. The first is to establish rules and contingencies that apply to *each* member of the class. That is, the same rule is applied to all members of the class, but the reward for adhering to the rule can be individually earned. For example, Mr. Rockwell was having difficulty with the noise level in his 45-minute study hall class. He informed his students that they were not permitted to talk in class. To determine whether they adhered to the rule, he divided the 45-minute class period into 5-minute intervals. Each student who was quiet during seven of the first eight 5-minute intervals (35 of the first 40 minutes) was excused for lunch 5 minutes early. A system designed in this way has the advantage of individualizing rewards so that each student who abides by the rule is reinforced. However, the disadvantage is that it requires diligent monitoring of students and may not be feasible when a teacher is simultaneously involved in teaching activities.

A second approach is to establish rules and contingencies that apply to *all* members of the class. In this case, a rule is established for all members of the class, and rewards are earned only if all members of the class adhere to the rule. For example, to apply this system in Mr. Rockwell's study hall class, all of the students would need to be quiet during seven of the first eight 5-minute intervals. All of the students in the class would then be excused 5 minutes early for lunch. However, if all of the students were not quiet during the required intervals, none would be able to leave early for lunch. This approach has the advantage of requiring less monitoring. Mr. Rockwell need not monitor to determine which student in the class was talking. He can simply continue his activities while listening for any talking. Another advantage of this approach is that peers often prompt or remind one another to work quietly. However, it may also have the negative effect of causing unwanted peer pressure. If peers apply undue pressure to their classmates, the potential for social difficulties is increased. When this occurs, an alternative approach should be used.

Question 15

> What is a potential disadvantage of applying contingencies to the class as a whole?

Conclusion

There are many preventive measures that can help reduce unwanted talking and noise in the classroom. In addition, simple reminders can assist students in learning classroom expectations. However, if talking and noise remain a problem with these standard approaches in place, a classroom intervention can be designed to ensure a quiet and productive learning environment.

PART IV:
Individual Interventions

Reward Systems

Disruptive classroom behavior can often be attributed to a few students or even a single student. In such cases, individualized interventions can be tailored to match students' needs, making them efficient and effective.

There are several approaches to individualized systems of behavior management. Reward systems are generally the best option because they allow a student to earn a reward for appropriate behavior. They set up positive interactions between a teacher and a student, and they focus on teaching the student desirable behavior.

The first step in designing a reward system is to define behavior the student should exhibit. For example, desired behavior might be "work quietly in class" or "use appropriate language." When defining desired behavior, it is critical that the student clearly understands what is expected. For some students this will require specificity. "Appropriate language" may need to be accompanied by specific examples, including "refrain from using curse words, use a quiet volume, and make sure no one else is talking when you join a conversation."

After defining desirable behavior, the next step is to determine the duration for which the student must engage in the behavior to earn a reinforcer. This should be individualized, depending on the age of the student and the frequency of undesirable behavior. Younger students generally need to be rewarded frequently; older students usually are able to wait longer for a reward, such as a class period or the entire school day. The frequency of behavior should also be considered when determining reward intervals. Behavior that is ongoing (e.g., happens approximately every 5 minutes) will require a brief reinforcement interval, while low-frequency behavior (e.g., one or two times during a 45-minute class) can be subject to a longer interval (e.g., a class period).

The next step is to select an appropriate reward. Guidelines described in Part II, Specific Setting Interventions, should be followed. This includes individualizing the reward to ensure it is preferred and something the student will work to earn, offering an array of options, and ensuring the reward is age appropriate. In addition, the quality of the reward must be weighed against the expectations. For example, offering an elementary-age student 5 minutes of free time at the end of the day for working quietly during all academic periods is probably not sufficient. Five minutes of free time at the end of the period may be more equitable. Finally, it is best if reinforcers are natural or logically linked to the desired behavior. Natural reinforcers are those that typically occur in a given situation, and they ensure that behavior will continue to occur without any preplanning. Examples of natural reinforcers in the classroom setting are praise, privileges, and free time. Examples of reinforcers linked to desired behavior are free time to socialize for a student who has difficulty refraining from chatting with friends or lunch with the teacher for a student who frequently calls out for the purpose of gaining teacher attention.

Along with selecting reinforcers, the teacher must determine the schedule of delivery. For younger children, reinforcers usually need to be delivered immediately. For example, 3 minutes of free time can be provided immediately after a student has worked quietly for 15 minutes. Older students are able to wait longer for reinforcers. Therefore, it is often more convenient to use symbolic indicators of their earnings, such as points or tokens, that can be accumulated to be spent during designated times throughout the day. For example, students may cash their points in for items at a school store. Tokens can be exchanged for special activities, such as playing computer games during study hall.

Question 16

> Why are systems that reward good behavior preferred over other types of behavior management systems?

_____

_____

_____

Behavioral Contracts

Behavioral contracts document an arrangement made between a teacher and a student. They are generally developed jointly and result from student–teacher negotiation. Contracts should state the expected behavior in positive terms, the conditions in which the behavior is expected, and the reward for meeting the terms of the contract. The contract should be signed by the teacher and the student and dated. When developing a contract, it is important that it is written so that a student can be successful. Figure 1 is an example of Ian's contract for quiet behavior.

QUIET BEHAVIORAL CONTRACT

Ian will work quietly during morning independent seatwork time.

Each day Ian works quietly, he will earn lunch with Mr. Cohen.

We agree to this contract:

Ian   Mr. Cohen   Date

_____   _____   _____

Figure 1. Ian's behavioral contract.

Question 17

What should a behavioral contract contain?

_____

_____

_____

Response Cost

Response cost systems involve fining students for misbehavior and are best used in conjunction with a reward system. For example, in addition to rewarding students with a point every 5 minutes for working quietly, one or several points can be deducted for talking out. Deducting minutes of recess time for students who talk out during quiet time is another example of a response cost. This added procedure sometimes makes a reward system more powerful.

There are a few cautions that need to be considered before using a response cost system. First, removing a reinforcer can make a student very angry, particularly when it is a tangible item, and the potential for a negative student reaction should be considered. Second, in order to remove a reinforcer, the student must have a pool from which to draw. For example, even if students earn points throughout the day for working quietly, they may not have accumulated sufficient points to compensate for points they lost for an early morning infraction. The system may need to be designed so that students are given a small pool of beginning reinforcers in the morning. Third, the amount of the fine must be carefully deliberated. If the fine is so large that a single infraction depletes a whole day's worth of earnings, students will lose their motivation to earn. A final consideration is what to do in case a student has lost all of his or her reinforcers. This leaves a teacher with no management system and the student without possible incentives. It can be avoided by weighing the frequency of misbehavior against the frequency of reward distribution. Another option is to allow the student to retrieve lost reinforcers for good behavior.

Question 18

List four cautions when using a response cost system.

a. _____

b. _____

c. _____

d. _____

Self-Management

Self-management is a procedure in which students are taught to manage their own behavior. Usually, students are taught to observe their own behavior throughout preset periods of time (e.g., 5-minute intervals) and then note, usually in written format, whether or not that behavior was appropriate (i.e., whether they followed certain preestablished expectations). Self-management can be a very effective individualized intervention for several reasons. It is often difficult for teachers to continuously monitor a student's behavior, particularly when they are teaching. Self-management does not require ongoing teacher surveillance. In addition, self-management requires that the student monitor his or her own behavior rather than relying on the teacher. This generally results in greater independence and, ultimately, self-control on the part of the student.

Question 19

> Describe two advantages self-management systems have over teacher-administered behavior management systems.

a. _____

b. _____

The initial step in developing a self-management system is to define the desirable behavior that the student will monitor. As described earlier, behavior should be defined clearly so that the student knows exactly what is expected. For example, "working quietly" might be defined as "working without talking unless given permission to talk by the teacher."

The next step is to develop a self-management device, which is simply a method for the student to record whether or not the desirable behavior occurred. The device is usually a preprinted card with a statement describing, in positive terms, the behavior the student will self-manage. For example, the card might state, "I was quiet." Written in the first person, the statement requires that the student record a response indicating whether or not the desired behavior occurred. For example, the student can simply circle "yes" or "no" in response to the statement, "I was quiet." An example of Kristin's self-management device can be seen in Figure 2.

Next, the student must determine the length of the intervals during which he or she will manage behavior. This will depend on the age

SELF-MANAGEMENT SHEET

Date: _____   Class: _____

Interval

1	I was quiet.	yes	no
2	I was quiet.	yes	no
3	I was quiet.	yes	no
4	I was quiet.	yes	no
5	I was quiet.	yes	no
6	I was quiet.	yes	no
7	I was quiet.	yes	no
8	I was quiet.	yes	no
9	I was quiet.	yes	no
10	I was quiet.	yes	no

Figure 2. Kristin's self-management sheet.

of the student and the frequency of the desirable or undesirable behavior. Because older students typically possess better self-control skills, intervals can be longer than for young students. Students who engage in high-frequency behaviors (e.g., talk out often) generally need to manage their behavior during brief intervals. The interval duration can be gradually increased as appropriate behavior increases. A timing device will be needed to signal the end of an interval. Tape recorders or watches that can be set to beep make good timing devices.

After the preliminary steps have been completed, the student needs to be taught to self-manage. Training consists of teaching the student to recognize the target behavior by modeling examples. The student then is taught to use the self-management device. During training, self-monitoring intervals might need to be shortened to expedite the process and ensure that the student is successful. Once the student is competent and successful, the interval duration can be increased.

After the student can accurately self-manage in the training context, he or she is ready to begin self-managing in the regular context. Initially, it is good practice for the teacher to simultaneously monitor the student's behavior and to conduct periodic checks to see that responses match. This will ensure that the student understands the procedures and is honestly self-managing.

Although self-management procedures alone are sometimes effective, it is generally advisable to provide rewards for achieving a pre-established criterion that is based on the frequency of behavior prior to self-management and ensures student success. For example, if a student typically talks out an average of every 6 minutes (five times during a 30-minute reading class), a reasonable interval length would be 5 minutes, and the student could be rewarded for refraining from talking out during three of the 5-minute intervals. After the student met this criterion for a week, it could be increased so that the student would need to refrain from talking during four of the 5-minute intervals to receive a reward. Increases should be very gradual to ensure that desirable behavior continues.

Question 20

Describe the steps for developing a self-management program.

a. _____

b. _____

c. _____

d. _____

e. _____

Conclusion

When problematic behavior is limited to only a few students in the classroom, intervention should be aimed at the individual. There are several different types of individual behavior management systems that can effectively reduce unwanted behavior and increase desired behavior. An individualized behavior management system should meet the needs of a student and be compatible with the teacher's preferences and the classroom environment.

FINAL EXAMINATION

1. How do students know what type of talking is acceptable in your classroom?

   _____

   _____

   _____

   _____

2. How do students in your classroom get permission to talk? What happens when they do not follow the rules?

   _____

   _____

   _____

   _____

3. Name three settings in your school and describe what type of talking is appropriate in each.

   a. _____

   b. _____

   c. _____

4. Describe the specific settings in your school where excessive or inappropriate talking and noisemaking occur.

   a. _____

   _____

   What information helped you identify these settings?

   b. _____

   _____

5. What is a universal rule that is appropriate for your school?

   a. _____

   _____

   How should this rule be applied to one of the specific settings that you identified as problematic in Question 4?

   b. _____

   _____

6. What are the three steps for teaching expectations for specific settings?

   a. _____

   b. _____

   c. _____

7. Describe three factors that can influence the success of a reward system.

   a. _____

   b. _____

   c. _____

8. What are the advantages of consequences that are logically related to the infraction or are instructive to the student?

   _____

   _____

   _____

9. How can good surveillance in specific school settings reduce problems?

   _____

   _____

   _____

10. List three physical features of a classroom that will reduce unwanted noise.

    a. _____

    b. _____

    c. _____

11. Describe three ways to prevent behavior problems in the classroom.

    a. _____

    b. _____

    c. _____

12. What is a signal you could use in the classroom to remind students to be quiet?

    _____

    _____

    _____

13. What is the difference between simple correction and positive practice overcorrection?

    _____

    _____

    _____

14. Describe a strategy to ensure that students are actively engaged.

    _____

    _____

    _____

15. What is a potential disadvantage of applying contingencies to the class as a whole?

    _____

    _____

    _____

16. Why are systems that reward good behavior preferred over other types of behavior management systems?

_____

_____

_____

17. What should a behavioral contract contain?

_____

_____

_____

18. List four cautions when using a response cost system.

   a. _____

   b. _____

   c. _____

   d. _____

19. Describe two advantages self-management systems have over teacher-administered behavior management systems.

   a. _____

   b. _____

20. Describe the steps for developing a self-management program.

   a. _____

   b. _____

   c. _____

   d. _____

   e. _____

ANSWER KEY

1. Answers will vary but may include teaching and talking about rules or hanging a poster delineating the rules in the classroom.

2. Answers will vary but may include raising hands or putting a card on their desk. Consequences for not following the rules could include giving a warning or loss of recess time.

3. Answers will vary but may include the following:
   a. cafeteria: whisper voice
   b. recess: outdoor voice
   c. hallways: quiet voice

4. a. Answers will vary but may include lockers, recess, and cafeteria.
   b. Answers will vary but should describe the informational source, such as direct observation; reports from volunteers, students, or school staff; or excessive disciplinary actions administered.

5. a. Answers will vary but should include a broad rule, such as, "Use an appropriate voice volume" or "Be respectful of others."
   b. Answers will vary but should reflect characteristics of the setting.

6. a. Establish rules based on expected behavior.
   b. Teach students the rules and how they should be applied in different settings.
   c. Practice the rules in context with reminders and feedback.

7. a. Rewards should be preferred and powerful so that students will want to earn them.
   b. Rewards should be periodically varied.
   c. Rewards should be age appropriate.

8. Students are more likely to find logical or instructive consequences acceptable because they make sense and they can teach the student a more appropriate way to respond in similar situations.

9. Good surveillance can function to prevent problems, remind students of good behavior, and enforce school rules.

10. a. Physically separating students from one another will decrease the noise level.
    b. Teacher observation and proximity will reduce inappropriate behavior.
    c. Designating a physically separate, nondistracting work area will decrease noise.

11. Behavior problems can be prevented by
    a. ensuring that the curriculum is interesting and challenging
    b. seeing that students understand classroom routines and lesson instructions
    c. providing stimulating activities for students when they complete their work

12. Answers will vary but may include providing a hand gesture, sounding a bell, or flashing the lights.

13. Simple correction requires that students practice appropriate behavior only once, and positive practice overcorrection requires that students practice appropriate behavior several times.

14. Answers may include choral responding, using individual chalkboards or dry-erase boards, or using cards with preprinted answers.

15. A potential disadvantage of group contingencies is that students may apply undue peer pressure on their classmates.

16. Rewarding good behavior sets up positive interactions between a teacher and a student and keeps the teacher focused on teaching desirable behavior.

17. Behavioral contracts should contain the behavior expected, the conditions in which the behavior is expected, and the reward for meeting the terms of the contract.

18. a. A student may become angry when a reinforcer is removed.
    b. To remove a reinforcer, students must have a pool from which to draw.
    c. The amount of the fine must be balanced against the infraction.
    d. Plans must be made so that students do not lose all of their reinforcers.

19. a. Self-management systems do not require continuous teacher monitoring.
    b. Self-management systems teach students independence and self-control.

20. a. Define the behavior.
    b. Develop a self-management device.
    c. Determine the self-management interval.
    d. Teach the student to self-manage.
    e. Introduce self-management in the natural context.

FURTHER READING

Alberto, P. A., & Troutman, A. C. (1999). *Applied behavior analysis for teachers.* Upper Saddle River, NJ: Merrill.

Axelrod, S., & Hall, R. V. (1999). *Behavior modification: Basic principles.* Austin, TX: PRO-ED.

Dunlap, L. K., Dunlap, G., Koegel, L. K., & Koegel, R. L. (1991). Using self-monitoring to increase independence. *Teaching Exceptional Children, 23,* 17–22.

Shapiro, E. S., & Cole, C. L. (1994). *Self-management interventions for classroom behavior change.* New York: Guilford Press.

Sprick, R., Garrison, M., & Howard, L. (1998). *CHAMPs: A proactive and positive approach to behavior management.* Longmont, CO: Sopris West.

Wong, H. K., & Wong, R. T. (1998). *How to be an effective teacher: The first days of school.* Mountain View, CA: Harry K. Wong.

ABOUT THE AUTHORS

Lee Kern, PhD, is an associate professor of special education at Lehigh University. Her interests are primarily in the areas of challenging behaviors, social skills, and self-management. She has published numerous research studies and book chapters on the topics of assessment and intervention for children with emotional and behavioral disorders and autism, including functional behavioral assessment, curriculum design, and social skills interventions. She serves on six editorial boards in the area of disabilities and special education and is associate editor for *Education and Treatment of Children* and *Journal of Behavioral Education.*

Gabriell Sacks, MA, is a doctoral student in special education at Lehigh University. She has worked as a classroom teacher with various age groups and with students with a variety of special needs. Her primary interest is working with students with emotional and behavioral disorders and their teachers in classroom settings.

Credit Card/PO Billing Address

Name _____

Address _____

_____

_____

_____

Ship To: Telephone Number _____

Name _____

Address _____

_____

_____

_____

GUARANTEE

All products are sold on 30-day approval. If you are not satisfied, you can return any product within 30 days. Please contact our office to receive authorization and necessary shipping instructions for returns. Prepaid orders will receive prompt refund, less handling charges. **Please use our fax number (1-800-FXPROED or 1-800/397-7633)!**

PAYMENT: All orders must be prepaid in full in U.S. funds by check or money order payable to PRO-ED, Inc., or by credit card. Open accounts are available to bookstores, public schools, libraries, institutions, and corporations. Please prepay first order and send full credit information to open an account.

Billing Authorization (must be completed or we cannot bill)

Purchase Order Number _____

❑ **Payment Enclosed**

Credit Card ❑ VISA ❑ MasterCard ❑ AMEX ❑ Discover

NOTE: Credit card billing address at top left must be completed if your order is charged to a credit card.

Authorized Signature _____

Card Number _____

Expiration Date _____

If prices on your order are incorrect, we reserve the right to exceed the amount up to 10% unless otherwise stated on your order. Terms are net, F.O.B. Austin, Texas; prices are subject to change without notice. ALL ORDERS MUST BE PAID IN U.S. FUNDS.

Quantity	Prod. No.	Book Title	Unit Price	Total
	10467	*How To Help Students Remain Seated*	$ 9.00	
	10468	*How To Deal Effectively with Lying, Stealing, and Cheating*	$ 9.00	
	10469	*How To Prevent and Safely Manage Physical Aggression and Property Destruction*	$ 9.00	
	10470	*How To Help Students Complete Classwork and Homework Assignments*	$ 9.00	
	10471	*How To Help Students Play and Work Together*	$ 9.00	
	10472	*How To Deal with Students Who Challenge and Defy Authority*	$ 9.00	
	10473	*How To Deal Effectively with Whining and Tantrum Behaviors*	$ 9.00	
	10474	*How To Help Students Follow Directions, Pay Attention, and Stay on Task*	$ 9.00	
	10475	*How To Deal Effectively with Inappropriate Talking and Noisemaking*	$ 9.00	
	10465	All 9 *How To* titles	$63.00	

Product Total _____

Handling, Postage, and Carrying Charges
(U.S. add 10%; Canada add 15%; others add 20%. Minimum charge $1.00) _____

Subtotal _____

Texas residents ONLY add 8.25% sales tax or WRITE IN TAX-EXEMPT NUMBER _____

Grand Total (U.S. Funds Only) _____